Big-norance

Dennis Boyd Call

ISBN: 9798669940768
Imprint: Independently published

DEDICATION

Dedicated to those people who actively work to improve the world through non-violent means ... they who are not looking for acclaim or notoriety, but who are sincerely more concerned about their fellowmen than themselves.

CONTENTS

ACKNOWLEDGMENTS

I must acknowledge my six children, all grown with families of their own. I look to them as examples of the things I write; it is particularly true of the topic of this book. Camielle, Bruce, Denalee, Michael, Jennilyn and Darryn: I love you!

1   DEFINING IT

Bignorance: *bigotry born out of ignorance and pride* (Dennis Boyd Call)

Bigotry: *obstinate or intolerant devotion to one's own opinions and prejudices* (Merriam Webster Dictionary)

Bigotry: *intolerance towards those who hold different opinions from oneself* (Oxford Dictionary)

Ignorance: *lack of knowledge, education, or awareness* (Merriam Webster Dictionary)

Ignorance: *lack of knowledge or information* (Oxford Dictionary)

Will Rogers is quoted as saying, "I never met a man I didn't like." That is fine as far as it goes. It is a very benign statement, but it makes me wonder about the context and venue.

The full statement attributed to him is this, *"I joked about every prominent man of my time, but I never met a man I didn't like."*[1] Still a rather benign statement, but it does create a slight alteration

---

[1] Quotesfromthepast.com

of perspective. Was he explaining some off-hand remark? Or being the humorist that he was, could it have been part of a routine? Does it make a difference? Not to me, because I love Will Rogers and his pragmatic outlook on life, politicians, and self-deprecating humor.

The point of this little exercise is this: So very often we only have partial knowledge of a given topic, movement or action. We then, with that little piece of fact (or maybe just someone's opinion), make judgments that could possibly be one hundred eighty degrees opposed to the truth.

A personal experience dramatically illustrated this operational viewpoint to me many years ago.

A gentleman whom I had known for only a few weeks was in my office for a consultation. We had plenty of time so we enjoyed getting to know each other better. Our conversation turned a bit political, discussing the various personalities and attributes of several candidates for a particular office.

My friend commented three times about one person's religion saying, "He cannot win because he has this Mormon thing about him."

Following the third time, I held up my hand to halt the conversation and said, "Before one of us gets our feelings hurt or anything of the sort, you should know something … I am one of them."

His facial expression was one of shock and disbelief. "You are? You are a Mormon?" he exclaimed.

"Yes," I replied. "I am, but I don't understand your feelings against my faith."

He looked quizzically at me as he said, "We don't hear many good things about the Mormons at my church." He fumbled around, making some comment about being Christian. He was clearly at a loss for words.

I assured him that we are indeed Christians. "In fact," I said, "Mormon is a nickname that was applied in the early days of the Church more than a hundred fifty years ago."

I continued, "The nickname came about because of the Book of Mormon, which we consider to be additional scripture. The true name of the Church is 'The Church of Jesus Christ of Latter-day Saints' which pretty much says it all."

His closing remark on the subject was, "Are you telling me that I should not believe everything that I hear from the pulpit?"

It then became a laughable situation between us. It has now been many years and we have since become the very best of friends.

I share this story because it typifies how bias, prejudice and bigotry can be generated, thus the word *bignorance*. The situation began innocently and ended in a great bonding experience for both of us. However, had it not been addressed at the start, it could have escalated to a level of bignorance unmanageable by either of us.

My story is just a microcosm of much worldwide bitterness, hatred and feelings of superiority. In this little Quick-Read we will discuss matters of race, religion and personal relationships, and the ugliness of *bignorance*.

2 PERSPECTIVES

It has been my observation that when an individual does something, it is because he has a reason. Tom may react to a given situation in one manner and David might react differently. And yet, Kathy may have a third reaction.

There may be three different conclusions and results; or the outcome may be the same in all three cases. Who used the correct process? Was one of these three people more correct than the other two? The big question however, may be: Why did they react in different ways? or, Why did they not all react exactly alike? Better yet, you may ask, *What difference does it make?* By asking that question, you have uncovered the total theme, plot and intent of this book.

Enlarging on that question, one could expand it to ask, Why are we sometimes adamant that a given method is the *only* way to resolve an issue? Or what makes one neighborhood more desirable than another? I have heard it said that particular postal ZIP codes are more desirable than others. Why should that be so?

Moving the question out of the neighborhood and into the community, it becomes a bit more complex. But the same basic issues are there.

What gives one community advantage over another? Are public services more important than public schools? Would it be right for one community to exclude nursing homes from within its boundaries, thus seeming to demean another community that accepts such facilities?

Continuing in our little societal journey, we come to our states. My family and I have lived in six of our United States. I have been asked which is my favorite. That is a difficult question because every state has its own attractions and qualities, as well as negative aspects. Given my limited knowledge, there are states wherein I would prefer to not live. Does that make those folks who do live there any less desirable?

As we further expand this adventure, it becomes imperative that we look at our nation as a whole. We are comprised of fifty states, over three thousand counties, and innumerable cities and towns. Is one jurisdiction more important than another?

Politicians seem to think so. But, just like Tom, David and Kathy, is it possible that the politicians are on different paths to the same destination?

If so, does that make any of the politicians bad people or less important? I think not! Diversity is what makes us a great nation.

Worldwide, the United States is envied, admired, loathed, scorned and reviled. People leave their native countries, risking their lives and the lives of their children in order to gain access to America, the "land of the free."

Certainly our freedom is the envy of the world, but does that make us, as humans, any better or worse than any other people? It sometimes seems that America has a target on its back. Despots try their best to undermine and destroy us. Why? Do we or don't we have a right to defend ourselves and our borders?

There are many aspects of the topic that are seemingly without answer.

The first section of this book takes a look at each of the scenarios mentioned above and listed below:

1) Tom, David and Kathy
2) The neighborhood
3) The community
4) The state
5) The nation
6) The world

Each person in our beautiful country is important! Individuals make the neighborhood and neighborhoods make the community. Communities comprise the state, the states make the nation and nations make the world.

It is true that as we transition our points of reference from one entity to the next (state to nation, etc.), our individual influence becomes more and more diluted because of the sheer number of people. That is one reason why we, in the United States of America, choose representatives to serve in our government.

This book is not a referendum on politics, but it does recognize the importance of understanding at least one key point of our system. That key point is the importance of the Electoral College.

In recent years we have had presidential elections wherein a particular presidential candidate won the popular vote, yet lost the election. Following the loss, many uninformed (ignorant) people, and even the candidate himself rallies a cry of unfairness.

"Unfair! unfair!" they vehemently assert. *"The majority of Americans wanted so-and-so but the other guy won because of the Electoral College."*

While the politicians themselves probably know better, they encourage this bellicose behavior. I believe they are hoping to either unseat the winner or simply have somewhere to place blame for their loss.

I do not know if our founding fathers realized how pivotal the College would be, but I believe they were inspired of God to insert this important feature into our electoral system.

Returning to my statement that each person in our wonderful country is important, this one component of our electoral system recognizes that fact.

The Electoral College membership reflects, in numbers, the exact count of senators and representatives of each state, plus three members who are duly elected from the District of Columbia.[2]

It is important to understand that they are *not* the same people as those serving in Congress, and meet only once every four years for the sole purpose of choosing our next President of the United States.

The rationale is that the balance of equality, equity and fairness is upheld. This was an evolving process within the deliberations of the founding fathers. There were proposals and rejections, the most workable and fair solution emerging as the Electoral College.

To further understand and appreciate the makeup of the College, it is important to understand the composition of Congress. But first, one must realize that the demographics of our lower forty-eight states are key to this conversation.

Our population is very heavily weighted on the east coast, as it is on the west coast. Mid-America, the breadbasket of America, is

---

[2] Archives.gov

less heavily populated, but provides the majority of our farmland, the great source of our basic need … food. Without our immense ability to provide nourishment for ourselves, as well as export a great deal to other countries, we would be quite a forlorn nation.

The President of the United States holds great power and influence, and that is as it should be. However, Congress collectively also has immense power and influence.

Here is the most impressive thing about our congress: Every state is allowed two Senators (equal representation per state). The House of Representatives, however, is *population* based.

While the total number of senators equals one-hundred, we have four hundred thirty-five representatives, the preponderance being from the heavily populated east and west coasts. Thus, the vastness of our population has fair and equitable representation in Congress.

This inspired method allows the recognition of sparsely populated states in the vitally important "breadbasket" states of mid-America.

It gives equal importance and consideration to everyone, that is, to each individual in the United States of America. Thus, while Congress and the Electoral College are similar in composition, they have no connection in function.

Unfortunately, as politically influential people seek to challenge the Electoral College, there is much bignorance demonstrated in their behavior.

They are uninformed, untruthful or selfish. (Or perhaps a combination of the three.) As a result, their voices are raised to falsely proclaim that mid-America should *not* have a voice in choosing our President. They certainly do not use those words, but that is their meaning. These people are practicing bignorance by their words, actions and spurious intent.

It is probably true that under any electoral circumstance, someone will be unhappy with the result and another display of bignorance would appear.

For example: Assume the Electoral College were eliminated and our President chosen by popular vote. The candidates would most certainly alter their tactics. They would likely campaign only in the most populous states; the voice of heartland-America is left to the mercy of banking and trade industry-America, thus creating a very egregious form of bignorance.

The system as we have it, not only encourages, but almost *demands* that our presidential candidates campaign in the less populated states of Mid-America. This is as it should be.

Let's take a look at a very logical metaphor. The 1996 World Series of baseball presents an interesting parallel. As you know, the Series is designed to accommodate a maximum of seven games. However, it is possible for one team to win the first four games, thus eliminating the final three games ... or consider the scenario below. The New York Yankees were pitted against the Atlanta Braves in the 1996 World Series.

Game one was won by the Atlanta Braves, 12-1. Game two was even a more severe hit (percentage-wise) against the Yankees. The Braves won 4-0.

In game three the tables were turned and the New York Yankees beat the Braves 5-2, followed by a similar victory in game four, the Yankees winning by a score of 8-6. At this point, the Series was tied.

Game five was a definite nail-biter, but New York pulled the rabbit out of the hat and won the game by a scant 1-0. In game six the New York Yankees pulled off another squeaker by winning 3-2 and were declared the World Series Champions for 1996.

Remember, the rules of the Series are that the team which wins four games out of the total of seven is the Series winner. Thus, in 1996 the Yankees, having won 4 games, were declared the winner.

"But … but wait a minute," someone says, "Let's add up the total points scored by each team. That will identify the actual winner!"

In checking the total score (popular vote), the Braves actually did accumulate more runs than did the Yankees. But the system is designed to give equal weight to each game (state) via an equitable distribution to location, fans and abilities of the teams (Electoral College).

From another perspective, consider each of our fifty states as individuals; some are short, some tall, some heavy and some thin and undernourished. Some of our hypothetical group are African-American, some are European, some Asian; Native-Americans are included, as are representatives of many other ethnicities, faiths, gender, occupations and political affiliations.

This scenario is not unlike the formation of the United States of America. It was constructed of people from various nations of the world. They had different cultures. They had lived under various types of governing regimes, and they held varying theological beliefs.

When threatened by England to stop the imminent break from English control, they formed a union. They banded together under a common cause because of the need they had for cohesion against an invading system, from which many of them had escaped.

Back to our make-believe, multi-cultural state-individual – they form an alliance with each other. They name this alliance the United Persons of Somewhere. Should any of these persons be excluded from representation in the decision making process of our newly formed republic? I think not! Thus it is with our own USA.

We are each important! And for one group, or one person, to feel more important than another is a portrait of the ugliness of bignorance. This type of bignorance embraces the ignorance of another person's plight, the intolerance of another's skin color, and the bias toward another's religious faith.

Sure, we all make choices that lead us to different educational pursuits, careers and levels of income, but that does not make one soul more important than another.

As we go through this Quick-Read book, I hope to point out how bignorance impacts everyone's lives. I hope to help elevate understanding and compassion in someone's mind. I hope to improve my own interactions with others by writing this book, which will include input from friends from cultures and faiths other than my own.

There is nothing so unfair as unfairness itself. And to understand what is unfair, we must come to a common understanding of the background of every race, creed and culture – a very daunting task. So, how can we do that?

3   TOM, DAVID AND KATHY
THE INDIVIDUALS

The belief and reference to "class" distinction is to state that one who enjoys higher income and privilege is of a higher "class" than those who have fewer material goods. True, they are of a higher "income class" but they are no better than those of lesser affluence and education. Many of our founding settlers left their homelands in order to escape such distinction.

I grew up hearing this idiom from my Mom, *"You don't have to follow the crowd."* My Dad's version was, *"All roads don't always lead to Rome."* One day he passed to me a visual that I shall never forget. He said, *"Don't be afraid to dig a few ditches."* I soon figured out that it was my parents' way of saying that I should learn to think independently and that there is no such thing as "lower class."

But there was also a much deeper significance to these phrases. Although they were trying to teach that additional value to me, it was a meaning that I really didn't grasp until several years later in life when I had married, and Connie and I were on our own.

It was a rude awakening for us when, in early 1957 as very young parents, we were relocating from our rural Idaho home to southern

California. Looking for a home in a price range we felt we could afford, we met with a realtor to inquire about a particular area. He made a comment about it being an "open" development.

It took a while for me to realize what he was saying. As I later pondered on that experience, the deeper meaning of what my parents had been teaching me, some fifteen or so years previous, began to sink in: *Tolerance is a virtue, so develop it.*

While I had accepted the lesson of multiple, independent thoughts and ideas on a topic – that some are good and some are bad – I suddenly realized that I had missed the part about human biases.

My wise parents were teaching me that I am no *better* than any other person and that, *yes, I am important and so is everyone else*; and, I am no *less* important than anyone else. It makes no matter the skin color, cultural difference, language skill, faith or education, we are all children of the same God.

I have been an avid people-watcher all of my life and as such, I have learned a lot. I have learned a lot about myself and I have learned a lot about others. I have learned that despite our differences, we are the same.

The problem is that at times, someone privileged in some sort of manner, may put himself upon a pedestal of superiority. Let's consider a child who senses from his parents that they are more highly educated than most of his school chum's parents. This can quickly translate, in the child's mind, to thinking that his family holds greater importance than most others on the playground. That child has inherited an attitude of bignorance from his parents.

Exclusion is a horrible form of bignorance among humankind. It may not be education or wealth, but it may be a special needs child in the school. Because he is different, he is sometimes excluded, ridiculed and shunned.

Under the guise of humor, kids can be extremely cruel. Unfortunately, I think that in most cases, the parents have a great deal of culpability in that attitude.

So, that begs the question, how does one become guilty of bignorance? Or better yet, how can one *avoid* becoming infected with bignorance?

Let's consider our three hypothetical characters: Tom, David and Kathy. They are approximately the same age: pre-school.

They live and play in the same neighborhood and are the best of friends. Their parents are solid, middle class blue collar workers who socialize together periodically, Although they are of different faiths none of them has felt any pressure from the others; they just enjoy their time together.

Tom's heritage is European, whose ancestors helped settle America; they are Christian. David's ancestry is Israeli, his great-grandparents arriving in America just as the Second World War was beginning; they are Jewish. Kathy's family were brought to America as slaves from Africa, prior to the early days of the republic; her family is also Christian.

What a wonderful idyllic relationship these three children have! Even better for everyone if their current perceptions would continue throughout the remainder of their lives. It makes one wonder what could possibly go wrong.

Well, what could go wrong might be peer pressure, as they begin to mingle with children at school who did not have the same pre-school experience.

The grade school these three chums attend is predominately white, including the teaching and administration staffs. The majority faith of their school community is Christian.

The children become exposed to many ideas, actions and protocols that they had never before experienced. A few of the classmates seem distant to Tom because he liked to sit with Kathy during lunchtime.

David learned that he felt more comfortable being around the few other kids of Jewish faith because of statements that were offensive to him, made by some of the Christian kids.

Kathy sensed that her friend Tom was being pressured to abandon his friendship with her so as to ingratiate himself to those who looked more like him. She slowly gravitated to almost exclusive association with the handful of others who were of the same skin color.

As Tom, David and Kathy continued through the remaining twelve years of school in their hometown, they each pretty well established their personal identities. They remained friends, but a distance developed between them. This is not necessarily wrong, unless that distance is because of a learned bias.

By learned bias, I mean some words and phrases heard on the playground, and sometimes in the classroom. It might be that another child grew up in a home where a particular ethnic idiom was commonplace, the family not realizing just what those words meant or that they might be offensive to another. *This is classic bignorance!*

Taunts seem to go hand-in-hand with those who feel a superiority to another – or – someone who has a deep-seated inferiority complex. Such a person may feel that the only way to elevate himself is to tear down those around him. Ridicule, mockery and scorn are acts that are picked up somewhere along the way. They seem to be magnified in one who is pre-disposed to use such tactics as he becomes older … and bolder.

Those who are the victims of ridicule and mockery will endure until one of two things happens: Either they will develop such a worthless opinion of themselves that they fade into oblivion and hide from society, or they let hatred develop to the point of explosion. The resulting noise could have repercussions way beyond reason.

As our three heroes continued their education and progressed through grade school, middle school and high school, they all maintained their friendship with the others in the trio … but … they drift apart.

Kathy felt a sort of alienation from David and Tom. David learned that it is not "good" to allow very much Christianity into his soul, and was encouraged to "hang-out" with other Jewish kids. Tom, who seemed to be in the majority position given the demographics of the community, began to develop a "superiority" complex.

The childhood buddies maintained their friendship, but as age, advanced education, and employment entered their lives, they all felt more comfortable within their own "class" or "culture." Is that bad? Not necessarily; it depends on how well they are able to maintain their cultural objectivity.

4 THE NEIGHBORHOOD AND COMMUNITY

I sometimes wonder what would have been our societal fate had our small family in 1957 decided to purchase a home and locate in the "open" development in southern California. As we discussed the possibilities, a request came to us from family back in Idaho that we return for a period of two or three years.

The idea of buying a home in sunny California became a non-issue for us ... but the concept of an "open" development continued to bother both Connie and me. We felt that all developments should be open, if affordable. It just did not seem right that there was an intimation of segregation vs. integration on the basis of skin color. The real estate agent was not overt in his words or actions, but when I asked him what he meant by "open development" his hesitant search for an answer was a dead giveaway as to *his* bias.

Fast forwarding a few years with our hypothetical subjects, Kathy, Tom and David, we find them in much different circumstances. All are married with children of their own. Tom has become a construction company executive, Kathy's chosen profession is family dentistry, and David is an insurance agent with a local agency, representing a large national insurance company. They each are achieving success in their chosen fields.

As Tom worked his way up in the construction business, he had association with many people of varying backgrounds and experiences. Many of the men whom he had labored alongside displayed extreme racial biases in their language. It bothered Tom greatly to hear such language … at first.

However, the humorous stories and joking hilarity that followed eventually infected Tom and he ultimately began to engage in such verbal behavior himself. He unwittingly developed an attitude of superiority, being led by those of gross bignorance.

Tom's situation encouraged his new bignorance through his inability to stand up against his "neighborhood" peer pressure.

David, meanwhile, learned that in the world of sales, there is little room for intolerance if he wants to make his business grow and mature. However, he also learned early on that there was a sort of bias culture in his local agency: If a prospective client was of such-and-such persuasion, that particular prospect should be referred to an agent of the same persuasion.

In fact, on one occasion David revealed to a fellow agent, who was African-American, that he was working with an African-American prospect. We will call the second agent Philip.

Philip asked the name of the prospect, which David readily shared. At that point, Philip blew a gasket and said, *"That prospect belongs to me because she is one of ours! And besides that, she goes to my church! You are to turn the case over to me!"* Bignorance, in this case, was not only a personal shortcoming, it pervaded the agency "neighborhood."

Kathy graduated near the top of her class in dental school. She aced every exam and excelled in all aspects of her training. Her knowledge and people skills were well documented; and she proceeded to enter the workforce.

She decided to find a dental group to become associated with rather than build a private practice from scratch. Kathy knew the hiring process would be somewhat competitive because of the number of students in her class. Her professional acumen was on display and she was called back for second interviews; the possibilities for a job offer seemed endless. However, as sensitive and gratifying as the interviews were, she sensed that she was never considered the top applicant.

The area where she desired to be employed had several dental offices, but they were all Caucasian owned and operated. Never in her job search was her ethnicity mentioned or even alluded to, but she did sense some discomfort among those with whom she associated.

Finally, at a small dental office some distance from her home, Kathy landed a job with a marvelously accommodating dentist. He was of Hispanic extraction, and he had a dedicated clientele that crossed all ethnic lines.

Kathy was very happy in her work, but couldn't shake the feelings of alienation she developed during her job search experience. She began to form a degree of animosity toward those whom she felt may have held an unexpressed bias during her interviews.

She failed to recognize that there may have been attributes where other candidates excelled and she fell short. As a result, Kathy developed a self-imposed bignorance that may or may not have had solid merit.

A portion of the genesis of bignorance can easily be found in the following quote: *"With every step of our lives we enter into the middle of some story which we are certain to misunderstand."*[3]

---

[3] G.K. Chesterton

Our three subjects are victims of different stories that have the same result: Bignorance!

Tom, in his eagerness to not make waves with his co-workers, did not understand the impact of offensive talk. He came to embrace such trash; first he tolerated and absorbed, then converted his childhood goodness into a gross misunderstanding of humanity.

David, as innocent as he was, learned a practice that was *not* company protocol. What he learned was the greed of a senior agent who masked that greed through his own version of bignorance. David was intimidated into believing that cultural bias was a way of life in his chosen field.

Kathy fell into a classic trap that pervades bignorance. She harbored feelings that were not substantiated by any act committed by her interviewers. Not being hired may or may not have anything to do with the color of her skin, but she did not recall seeing any other black employees in any office. This fed into her thoughts, and she let it fester. Finally she allowed a possible misunderstood rejection to overcome her childhood naiveté.

So who is right and who is wrong in each of these situations? Well, I suspect that each character, no matter the side, would maintain his or her posture as being correct. Hence the following quote fits perfectly:

> *"Here lies the body of William Jay, - Who died maintaining his right of way. - He was right, dead right, as he sped along, But he's just as dead as if he were wrong.*
>
> *"You may be right, dead right, as you speed along in your argument; but as far as changing another's mind is concerned, you will probably be just as futile as if you were wrong."*[4]

---

5 THE STATE

It is interesting to me that each of our states has something it is noted for. The state of Idaho where I grew up is well known for its potato production. In fact, for many years the automobile license plates held the image of a baked potato in the center of the plate with the words "Famous Potatoes" clearly imprinted at the top of the plates.

The Idaho Russet potatoes were considered so wonderfully delicious because of the prime volcanic soil, the warm days, and the chilly nights of the area. Everyone knew that.

Therefore, I was almost offended when, sometime in my mid-teenage years, I discovered that the state of Maine was considered a primary source of potatoes. I had grown up learning of Idaho's dominance of the potato-growing industry. I thought, *"All of America knows that Idaho is the only place where spuds are grown. The acclaim belongs to us!"*

Having spent my youthful farm days planting, raising and harvesting spuds, I felt ownership, and thus dedication to and for the entire United States potato market! My bignorance showed!!

I had difficulty, however, because Idaho was called the "Gem State." In fact that was the state motto: The Gem State. I had not been taught of the multitude of gems found in the rich volcanic mountains; to me it was all about the spuds. I was a victim of bignorance and did not even realize it!

It broke my heart when Connie and I set out on the adventure of being newlyweds, moving to California where I received a severe cultural lesson. Some locals did not even know where Idaho was on the map, let alone have a clue as to how famous the Idaho Russet was!

Is this a simple analogy describing how bignorance can come into one's life? Certainly it is, but it represents how insidious it can actually become.

Similarly, we had been conditioned for generations that all politicians and business executives were to be male ... and white. When a black person was elected to a major city office it became national news. I was still a naïve Idaho farm kid, although living in southern California in 1967, when Carl Stokes from Cleveland, Ohio made headline news. I cannot say for certain, but I suspect that his accomplishment made him an international hit.

That was the year that Mr. Stokes, a black man, was elected Mayor of Cleveland. He was the fifty-first mayor of that major city and the news media headlined his accomplishment for days. I applauded his success, but felt how sad it was that the color of his skin is what brought him the fame ... on the other hand, I was glad that he had broken the barrier.

Since that red-letter event, there have been many African-American men and women who have distinguished themselves in the political arena. And they have not come from just one party.

The correlation between my Idaho spud story and the choice of Carl Stokes as an elected official of a major U.S. city is this: The expansion of knowledge, exposure and experience is a good thing.

It broadens one's awareness that all wisdom is not held within one single group or culture. It demonstrates that growing up in a sheltered environment may limit a person's ability to understand and relate to another's perspective.

Unfortunately, too often we fail to have our minds open enough to accept another point of view, and thus we shrug it off as not valid or just plain wrong. Here is where bignorance can become a danger. Pride rears its ugly head, it unites with ignorance, and the result is horrid bignorance that reveals itself at some point.

It becomes a flashpoint for arguments, fighting, even escalating into riotous behavior. Neither side of any issue will consent to discussion, compromise or friendship of any sort. This situation touches on the question in the second chapter of this book: "Why are we sometimes adamant that a given method is the *only* way to resolve an issue?"

One of the interesting things about America is the cultural division existing in identifiable geographical areas. Colin Woodward wrote, and asserts quite convincingly, that we are actually eleven rival regional cultures of North America. He says that these cultures are not just confined to the United States, but spill over into Canada and Mexico.[5]

As mentioned in Chapter 2, our union was formed to meet the need of common interests. The most pressing common need of the several different cultures at the time was the threat of destruction by England. They came together because of a need, but did that erase differences? Of course not. In a sense, it served to consolidate peoples of like cultures into one union; but it also laid a fertile groundwork for competitive behavior.

---

[5] American Nations by Colin Woodward

Competitive behavior is like a two-edged sword. Competition produces improvement in goods manufactured and sold, but at the same time competition can produce envy, distrust and one-upmanship. Nowhere is this more evident than in our United States of America today … and indeed, throughout the entire world.

The Dutch quite naturally tended to band together as did those of German descent. People of the Amish faith felt comfortable among their own … and on and on and on. Very comfortable colonies were formed and prospered on their own. In fact they even developed commerce between the different colonies.

We lived in southeastern Pennsylvania during the 1970s and early 1980s. We loved driving to the Amish country to partake of their fabulous eateries and to see the horse-drawn buggies traveling the roadway. It almost seemed like a step back in time to us, and especially to our children. Would I like to live in that culture? No. It was foreign to me, although we lived only two counties away.

Two hours to the south of our home at the time, was where the Capitol of our wonderful republic was located, Washington, D.C. Two to three hours north of our home was New York City, the financial center of most of the world.

So here we were, three different cultures, all within a few hours' drive from one another. Three different points of view as to what drives our successes. Personally, I would not like to live in, or be a part of, any of the three. I was very content with our rural-suburban lifestyle in Chester County, a fourth culture.

So what is my point in all of this? The point is that all of us are living in different circumstances with differing views and desires; in fact, differing cultures. Which of the many is best? All of them are good, and each of the people living within each culture has a different path to the same destination in life: To live well, to successfully raise our families (if we have them), and to retire at the appropriate time in comfortable circumstances.

As my mother said, *"You don't have to follow the crowd."* But the unsaid part of that statement is, *"Be tolerant of those who are the crowd, they probably hold differing views amongst themselves."*

I was given a very rude awakening several months ago when I posted on Facebook, a very small portion of an open letter that I had written to our members of Congress and the President of the United States.[6]

Actually there were two posts: The first addressed what I see as shortcomings in the behavior of Congress, along with some suggestions. The second post addressed the President, also with some suggestions.

Whether I am liberal or conservative, Republican or Democrat makes no difference to the message of this story. Following the first post, I received a half dozen comments which were rather benign and well stated. They neither attacked me nor individual persons in Congress. The comments were of observation and encouragement to do better, and for Congress to become more forthcoming with the truth, etc.

My second post addressed our sitting President, but not by name. I suggested that he "turn off the tweet machine" and look for the good in members of Congress who disagreed with him.

My post was immediately bombarded by a dozen or so individuals who called me names that I have never ever been called before. These alluded to the idea that I held a terrible political bias.

---

[6] If You Only Understood and If You Really Cared

I responded to only one of the comments in this way, "Perhaps you should read the book." The person's comeback was the reaction of one filled with bignorance, "I don't need to read your book. I know what you are!"

You see, we become so entrenched in our own dogma that anyone with whom we do not agree is wrong, and automatically becomes our enemy. Bignorance expands, name calling and put-downs become the norm, and ultimately, in the big picture, violence and anarchy can, and often does, take over.

We see bignorance displayed every day on our news channels and we read of it in the many social media posts available. It is presented with an indignity that exceeds all realm of responsible reporting. We are receiving mixtures of news and opinion; very little *reporting* of hard news is actually done.

Shades of anarchy are appearing across America and it seems that many of the people are involved because they have a desire to "follow the crowd" rather than think for themselves. Rather than work to improve on what *they* now have, they work to destroy what *others* have worked hard to achieve.

Sure, there is an element of bad in the world, but being *badder* is not the solution. Havoc and disorder are friends to those who would loot and plunder for their own gain.

Much damage is done under the guise of racial discrimination. Not that there isn't such a condition, because there are gross racial divides; but that is not a reason to cause mini-revolutions in our streets. Legitimate change takes time, but the anarchy route will take much longer to enact true change.

Mankind must learn to live by a higher code of ethics, a law of conduct that is for the common good, and a law that benefits people of every "class."

6 THE NATION

Colin Woodward's book, American Nations, has as the sub-title: "A History of the Eleven Rival Regional Cultures of North America." In it he states: *"I have very consciously used the term nations to describe these regional cultures, for by the time they agreed to share a federated state, each had long exhibited the characteristics of nationhood.*[7]

He further explains the differences between statehood and nationhood. Suffice it here to say that as he has identified the regions, one can see how the attitude of bignorance could have been developed regionally, among the people of the United States.

Being western born and raised, Connie and I had certainly developed a western mentality. Our oldest child was sixteen when we moved from southern California to southeastern Michigan. When our California friends heard where we were moving, several of them made this statement, *"Why in the world would you move to a place where they have all of those tornadoes?"*

Our new friends in Michigan similarly asked the question, *"Aren't you happy to have moved away from all of those earthquakes?"*

---

[7] American Nations p.3

Three years later, we moved to southeastern Pennsylvania. The Michiganders whom we knew and loved said, *"Really? You are going to the land of hurricanes?"*

Our experience in California was of a laid-back culture. A place of casual living where knowing a native born Californian was a rare happening; everyone it seemed, was born elsewhere and moved to California, creating a homogenous mixture of transplants. Our different backgrounds were what we had in common.

In southeastern Pennsylvania we experienced what was almost an opposite feeling. I made a comment to a person that it was not as easy to make new friends in Pennsylvania as it had been in California. Said he, *"Well, we easterners have been here three-hundred years and don't take to newcomers that easily."* The comment was not egregious in nature, but we sensed that we needed to take a new approach to making friends.

I recall one new friend who was very insightful; he took me aside one day. Having overheard a particular attempt at humor by me, he said, *"Dennis, people here do not understand your western sense of sarcastic humor. I suggest you tone it down a bit."*

Woodward alludes to the settling of the Far West by two groups:

One group – the Yankee Mormons of Utah – would found a distinct subculture of independent farmers in Utah and southern Idaho. The other – the gold-hungry Forty-niners – were highly individualistic frontiersmen in the Appalachian mold.

The Mormons ... Fleeing persecution in the Midwest in 1847 ... Almost all were from Yankeedom ...[8]

---

[8] American Nations, p. 245

Further examination of the topic of persecution of The Church of Jesus Christ of Latter-day Saints reveals bignorance of a gruesome nature. Earlier, Missouri had become a central gathering place for members of the fledgling religious organization.

Among other things, one of the strikes held against the Church by locals was the anti-slavery position held by those "Yankeedom" Mormons. In 1838, the governor of Missouri issued what has become known as the Extermination Order. The order stated that the Mormons were to be exterminated or driven from the state if necessary. The order was not officially rescinded until 1976.

In 1847, the center of The Church of Jesus Christ of Latter-day Saints was established in the future state of Utah. Thus, one culture had been driven from the midst of another culture, only to establish itself in a land that was unsettled, barren and climatically hostile.

As long as I can remember there has existed anti-Semitism. Sometime in the last couple of years, an attack on a synagogue killed a number of Jewish worshippers. Some friends of mine who hold true to their Jewish faith were traveling not too distant from where this horrible event occurred.

I felt impressed to send a text to my friends expressing my hurt, and personal disdain for the awful insidious act. His response was one of appreciation, and then he stated, *"Your people have suffered the same intolerance."*

By following the "births" of the eleven nations as described in Woodward's book, one can begin to understand how bignorance can creep into the psyche of most anyone. The challenge is to not blindly become bignorant, but to openly behave in such a manner as to accept the differences with understanding.

By being understanding and not behaving bignorantly, we can become further educated as to the uniqueness of other cultures. We can co-exist without rancor, put-downs or racial biases. I become delighted when I observe that a member of a minority group achieves prominence. Whether or not I agree with his or her politics or religious beliefs becomes a non-issue; that person has demonstrated strength, courage and an ability to rise above.

I find it exciting to learn about our differences. We can become educated well beyond expectation if we will only take the time to learn; and we learn by being taught. If we think we are always learning truth by simply observing and then making judgments, we will be way off the mark, and simply ingraining bignorance into our own hearts and minds.

But, on the other hand, if we become friendly conversants with others, our sincerity will be recognized and appreciated. Not only will friendships be solidified, but we will also be building a peace and unity rarely experienced anywhere.

7 THE WORLD

So we see that one's individual behavior influences the behavior of the neighborhood, community, state and nation. As each entity enters the picture, the magnitude expands exponentially. In a family and neighborhood, which is relatively small, we can actually see the impact of our individual actions. But as we move into larger groups, i.e., states and nations, one's positive (and sometimes negative) individual actions can become obscure and seemingly unimportant.

In fact, examining some people's attitudes reveals another aspect of bignorance. In our glorious United States of America one of our often overlooked and underestimated privileges is our right to vote.

Some say, *"My vote won't make a difference."* Or, *"They are all a bunch of crooks anyway."* By the very act of inaction through ignoring the voter's booth, one has surrendered a legitimate right. That is akin to believing that a private voice cannot make a difference in the neighborhood or community.

Carrying this thesis into the next realm of our expanding environment, the world, a single person's individual act is further diluted and diminished. But there are those who have risen above that attitude. Take for example, the leaders of any movement, religious or otherwise: Martin Luther King, Mother Teresa, Rosa Parks, and Nelson Mandela are examples of promoting non-violent cultural improvement. There was Martin Luther, Mohammed, Moses, Joseph Smith, and the ultimate: Jesus Christ, each of whom sparked a change for the betterment of mankind. If the word had been around in their time, their movements would have worked to crush *bignorance* in any form.

Below, I quote a beautiful prayer of peace which is often attributed to the Italian Saint Francis of Assisi. Although he may or may not have penned the words, it makes little difference. The words, intent and meaning go way beyond all bignorance. This prayer states just the opposite. In doing my research, I found a number of iterations of this prayer, all very similar.

An Anglican friend passed this on to me and I share it here with you.

The Prayer of Saint Francis of Assisi

Lord, make me an instrument of Thy peace;
Where there is hatred, let me sow love;
Where there is injury, pardon;
Where there is discord, union;
Where there is doubt, faith;
Where there is despair, hope;
Where there is darkness, light;
Where there is sadness, joy.
O Divine Master,
Grant that we may not so much seek
To be consoled, as to console;
To be understood, as to understand;
To be loved as to love.
For it is in giving that we receive;
It is in pardoning that we are pardoned;
And it is in dying that we are born to eternal life. Amen

The observations, the desires and the motivations expressed in this prayer should be non-denominational. They should be held in the hearts of every person born into this world.

One may legitimately counter the non-violent movements begun by the individuals named on the previous page and subsequent like-minded people. But in so doing, interlopers often take advantage and carry it too far, thus creating reactions of differing degrees of violence. It can be true that those who choose to not open their minds to the possibility of improved lives may be subject to involvement in unwarranted violence. That is the epitome of bignorance.

I have a saying: "Always keep an open mind, but be careful of what seeps in." We can learn so much good if we were to listen to others with the intent of learning. I have another saying: "Many people listen only to respond, not to hear." It is so sad, that some are so predisposed to prove themselves right that they fail to hear what the other person is actually saying.

This can be observed daily in the so-called news interviews on television. The host poses a question to the guest, and while the guest is answering, it is clear that the host is formulating an argumentative response. The clarity is especially obvious when the host keeps interrupting the guest, not allowing a full answer. While this is not true in every case, it is quite obvious much of the time. Here again, bignorance reigns in the mind and on the tongue.

I remember as a child, being sent outside by my mother with one of my siblings to settle an argument. She said, *"When you have come to a solution, you may come back inside."* Her method worked wonders!

Thus it could be with much of the world's inability to find constant peace. The best solution to many of the world's problems are not to the extreme right or left, it is somewhere in the middle. Much of the problem lies within the realm of bignorance on the part of differing nations.

Nations are made up of different states, (or sometimes influential groups), states made up of different communities, which are made up of different neighborhoods, which are made up of different individuals. Individually we can all make a difference by rising above bignorance and being an example of the beauty defined by the words in The Prayer of Saint Francis of Assisi.

If we all were to live by the above words, it would put a dagger into the very heart of bignorance; it would exist no more.

8   THE WORKPLACE

Very likely one of the most fertile areas for the nourishment of bignorance can be found in the workplace. It can begin when someone has made an infraction of the rules of a particular position and is disciplined for that breach.

Take for example our intrepid insurance agent, David. He had learned by example, from a senior agent named Philip, of a practice in the local agency. You may recall that Philip demanded that one of David's prospective clients be referred over to Philip because of race and faith issues.

This was in direct violation of the major insurance company policies that they both represented, but the *local* agency office apparently allowed such behavior. It had become their own local culture. But now, David has a full year's experience, and he is comfortable in his job … but he has another come-uppance.

A new agent, a nice lady by the name of Marsha, who is just getting her start in the insurance business, approaches David. Marsha tells David of a prospective client of the Jewish faith and asks David about the propriety of doing business during the upcoming Jewish holiday season.

David, remembering the lesson he had learned from Philip many months previous, responds with what he had assumed was accepted protocol. He says to Marsha, "You know that I am also Jewish and that any prospects of my faith belong to me. Please give all of the information you have regarding these folks to me and I will take care of them. They are *my* people!"

Stunned but accepting, Marsha does as she is instructed and brings her file on the prospective client to David's office within the hour.

The next morning, the agency manager invites David into his office and asks about his interaction with Marsha the day before.

David innocently replies, "She was beginning to work with some folks who are my people. We belong to the same faith and share a common heritage."

He further explains what transpired between him and Philip almost a full year prior. David shares that he had given, at Philip's demand, the files pertaining to some prospects that were of the same faith and ethnicity as Philip.

"Well," says the manager, "Philip is a senior agent in this office and is one of our very top producers. With more than twenty years of experience he has proven his value to the company and to this office.

"I will speak with Philip about the issue. In the meantime, I am putting you on probation for a year, effective today. If there is any further funny business in your actions, you will be terminated."

Was bignorance in play in the foregoing illustration? Absolutely! Philip was grossly bignorant by knowing that his tenure and high production numbers would allow him to get away with his demand from David, so he took advantage of his "superior" position. Pride was the major factor in Philip's bignorance. The manager enabled

Philip's bignorance through his own attitude and acceptance of the senior agent's actions.

What is David to do about the situation? He can do an end-run around his manager and bring it to the attention of upper management; he can confront Philip and demand some sort of compensatory satisfaction. He can become bitter and vow to get even with Philip over the coming months or years … as long as it takes. The only other option would be for him to resign and find employment with another company … but they will surely learn of his probationary status; that would certainly not work to his favor.

Actually, David chose none of the above. He, being a very bright, honest man chose to swallow his pride and make the best of his new double-edged education. David knew that he could continue to succeed in his business … feeling good about working with any newfound prospects, even those not of Philip's race and faith.

David understood that the problem was not his, but Philip's. He took the less traveled road, the high road, and forgave Philip; he eliminated it from his mind. David doubled down on his efforts and as a result his business exceeded all expectations.

Some of the most sad illustrations of personal bignorance occur in the healthcare field. Specifically, there have been cases where an attending nurse will take it upon himself or herself to end the life of a patient through medical means.

All too often we hear through news sources, of a caregiver who, perhaps out of misplaced compassion, will withhold medication … or … even just the opposite. Sometimes excess medication has been administered to the patient, causing their death. Bignorance reigns within these caregivers because of their authoritative attitude, as well as lack of respect and honor for the patient and family, no matter the compassion. Caregiver bignorance need not always be so criminally intense as just described, but can be rather benign, comparatively speaking.

We hear of patient neglect, such as not feeding the patient regularly, not giving proper bathroom attention, and allowing bedsores to form on patients. In short, patient neglect is a terrible form of bignorance because of the greed or laziness of the caregiver. They are more concerned about themselves and their own ease than the patient. Where else on earth should practicing The Prayer of Saint Francis of Assisi be more appropriate than in a home where a family's loved ones have been placed?

The employee to employer relationship in any work venue can hold both pleasantries and bignorance. Continuing with the healthcare scenario, I have heard of cases where duties were totally ignored. This because of apparent lack of respect toward the employer, as well as the patients involved. Having been involved with professional final-life care when my wife passed away, I am amazed at the high quality care she received by the nurses who attended her. But such is not always the case.

Another person's attending nurse took the attitude that since her patient was required to wear a diaper in her final months, there was no need to attend to the patient's bathroom needs preemptively. When the nurse's employer discovered the situation and discussed it with her, she was alarmed at the "higher-than-thou" attitude of the nurse. Indignity-induced bignorance ensued. She said, *"There was no need to be concerned because she wears a diaper, so that protects the bedsheets."* In her mind, the patient was not the important issue … the bedsheets were!

Willful failure by an employee to abide by company policy in any business can be a dangerous form of bignorance. It may put other employees at risk. It may even put the lifeblood of the entire company in jeopardy.

9 STEREOTYPES

"Have you heard the one about ...?" is probably one of the worst open displays of bignorance there is. It promotes stereotypes that are not true! Many years ago we were inundated with *Polish* jokes; more recently have been the *blonde* jokes. Irish, Catholic, Jewish, Black, Mormon and probably every nationality and religious faith have been used as the butt of jokes, which are intended to bring laughter about some distinct feature of that stereotype.

But stereotyping brings much more than gaiety into the equation. It introduces a false sense of superiority to the person who would engage in such trite verbal trash. Sure, some of the jokes may be hilarious, but at the expense of someone who is of that persuasion.

However, we must be able to laugh at ourselves as well. Polish jokes are very funny to me, partly because a percentage of Polish blood flows through my veins. So that is part of the dilemma; what is appropriate and what is carrying it too far?

From another perspective, and perhaps equally perplexing: Is it right for members of a certain group to refer to themselves in one fashion, and wrong for people outside of the group to use the same reference when speaking to, or of members of that group? Very much an unanswerable question to me ... except ... we should always try to be sensitive to others and to the possibility of offense.

Our politicians, at different times, have tried to limit access to the United States by people of certain faiths and nationalities. While there may or may not be a preponderance of people of a given persuasion that are undesirable, is it fair to broad-brush the entire culture? I have a problem with that. I have heard several people speak with disdain about Muslims; this because of the bignorance ingrained in their minds and hearts, brought about by the ugly behavior of a very vocal minority of people of that faith.

I have several good Muslim friends whom I hold in higher regard than some people of my own faith. One of them faithfully travels to Mecca every year. One year he purchased and brought home to me a large, beautiful picture of that place that is sacred to him and the entire Muslim world. It is one of my prized possessions and I am grateful for his friendship.

The extreme ugliest of the ugly in regards to discrimination has been demonstrated for centuries, I suppose. Attempts to try and justify the movement, it has been referred to as "ethnic cleansing." What the heck is that all about?!? Cleansed from what? Talk about a superiority complex! It is pure extermination and no legitimate softening phrase can be created. And the idea of devolving into the "master race" is so outlandish as to defy any and all logic. But it was attempted by the Nazis under the direction of Adolph Hitler.

The most egregious "ethnic cleansing" in my lifetime was the Holocaust during the World War II years. It is estimated that six million Jews were murdered at the hands of the Nazis during that time. But that was not the end for these persecuted people. Almost concurrently, another gross injustice was perpetrated against the Jews when tens of thousands were murdered at the hands of Joseph Stalin, the leader of Russia. There is no definitive number of Jewish people held in gulags or other labor camps, then murdered by Stalin; the smallest estimate I could find in my research was seventy-five thousand, but others claim a much higher number.

The side effects of the concentration camps of Germany and the labor camps of Russia extend way beyond the actual events. My wife and I lived in Canada for three years during the early 1990s. We became acquainted with a Jewish couple who had survived the concentration camp prior to making it to freedom in British Columbia. The stories they told were difficult to speak, but they also knew that verbalizing an experience was a good way to let it go, to find relief. My heart went out to these dear people as we listened to their heartfelt stories. But it was not until one particular experience that I gained a much clearer understanding.

Connie and I were visiting with this elderly couple in their home just before she was about to go to the kitchen to bring dinner to the table. She turned her back to us and began a slow walk. When she had taken only a step or two, I quietly caught up to her and laid my hand on her shoulder. I wanted to ask if I could help with dinner.

Surprised by immediately feeling my hand on her shoulder, she whipped around, her fist clenched and in motion toward my face. Almost as quickly, she caught her own hand and I recoiled from astonishment. She glared at me and said, *"Don't ever sneak up on me like that again. You are very fortunate that my fist did not make it to your face!"* Her husband was equally adamant in his reaction. He was at her side as quickly as possible holding his open hand toward me.

Catching his composure, this kind, understanding man said to me, *"That action to her is a sign that she is to be taken aside and to give herself to the guards. She was treated brutally. It is a subconscious reaction for her because it happened to her so many times in the camp."*

What an awful thing to have to live with for so much of her life; so many years of talent and grace nearly destroyed, driven by a societal hatred that goes way beyond bignorance!

As demonstrated, when taken to its extreme, bignorance through stereotyping can engulf entire generations, family heritages, nationalities, faiths and skin colors. Very notably in the stereotypical genre is the insidious notion that black people are of some inferior species. My good friends who are black have no more duty to excel than do I. Not having a formal education beyond high school does not bring ridicule or put-downs to me; neither should it bring ill treatment to them.

They are among the most loving, considerate and industrious people around. To hear, and occasionally see, any type of disparagement to their culture is offensive and uncalled for. The ancestry of many of them is the unfortunate circumstance of being brought to America as slaves. That was the ultimate display of ugly bignorance on the part of those who suffered a superiority complex. With that horrid complex they treated these "prisoners" as cheap collateral that could be bought and sold with impunity.

To demean this wonderful group of people in any fashion is to tell God that He made a horrible mistake. It is to deny that God our Father does exist, all the while inferring that Jesus Christ died in vain when He hung on that cross at Calvary. Nowhere in any scripture have I read that we are to shun any person, family or people because of skin color. But we are commanded to shun evil; and people, because of color, whatever it may be, are not evil! They are not to be the butt of jokes or inflammatory comments.

Of course there are people of color throughout the world who hold evil intent, but they certainly do not have a monopoly there. Evil intent is found in every nationality, culture and faith. It is individual in nature, and perhaps in clusters such as gangs, but not as a result of skin color.

I cringe when I hear or read of horrible events taking place in any part of our world, particularly in this, the United States of America.

And as I watch looting, rioting and uncontrolled behavior on the television news programs, I see people of both dark skin and light skin. Several recently viewed looting scenes involved people with white skin as well as black. But that is not pointed out by newscasters. It sometimes seems that only minority groups have the distinction of being noticed in these devastating events.

I will be most proud to stand alongside my friends of minority populations, as well as my wonderful white friends at judgment day.

10 WHEN WE ALL COME TOGETHER

Have you ever considered what a wonderful world it would be if there were no wars, no hatred, no envy or strife? It is my belief that sometime in the future this will happen. In the meantime, we have a lot to accomplish. Am I so naïve to think that one guy from Idaho can bring it about? No, of course not. But I also think that collectively we can accomplish a great deal by moving toward that direction. I learned in high school shop class that the load-bearing capacity of a vertical eight-foot 2x4 is about 800 pounds. But by nailing two eight-foot 2x4s together the capacity increases by almost 5 times.

A similar phenomenon can occur for good within the ranks of humanity. We can begin in our homes by eliminating bignorance in our personal lives. Then, the strength of many will be able to withstand and crush bignorance in our neighborhoods, reversing it as we learn to love those with differing political, religious and cultural beliefs. It will take personal commitment to act positively rather than react negatively to any given circumstance.

I am reminded of the Old Testament scripture: *"How beautiful upon the mountains are the feet of him that bringeth good tidings, that publisheth peace; that bringeth good tidings of good, that publisheth salvation; that saith unto Zion, Thy God reigneth."*[9]

---

[9] Isaiah 52:7

We are a long way from the utopia described above. But wouldn't it be wonderful if each of us were to live a life so worthy that our headstone could be inscribed with these words: "He (or She) made a difference"?

There have been a plethora of songs written about this topic. Standing out in my mind are the beginning words of the song "Lean on Me."

> Sometimes in our lives
> We all have pain, we all have sorrow.
> But if we are wise,
> We know that there's always tomorrow.
>
> Lean on me when you're not strong
> And I'll be your friend, I'll help you carry on
> For it won't be long
> 'Til I'm gonna need somebody to lean on.

One must wonder if peace is at all possible; can we overcome bias and prejudice? My answer is a definite yes! Of course I am not a social scientist, an anthropologist, or professional of any kind who can back-up my statement with research or data. However, I enjoy history and can point to contemporary successes.

For example, bitter enemies in World War II, the United States and Japan have reestablished peace, understanding and commerce. The same is true between the USA and Germany. Further back in history is the remarkable ally we have in the United Kingdom, the country that was the catalyst for the formation of our own union about two hundred fifty years ago.

The future for each of us will be what we make of it. Some will find peace and others will not; we become what we think and what we do. Great truths are found in some of the unlikeliest places:

Ella, aka Cinderella, had a memory of her mother's counsel, as she faced mistreatment from her wicked stepmother and stepsisters. This beautiful daughter, turned into a servant, arrives at a mindset wherein she determines to make the best of her sad situation. Her memory comes to mind as good advice for all of us as we move forward with life. Her loving mother had said, *"Ella, my darling. I want to tell you a secret, a great secret that will see you through all the trials that life can offer. You must always remember this, have courage and be kind. You have more kindness in your little finger than most people possess in their whole body. And it has power, more than you know. And magic."*[10]

---

[10] Brittany Candau, Have Courage, Be Kind: The Tale of Cinderella

ABOUT THE AUTHOR

Dennis Boyd Call grew up an Idaho farm boy near the small town of Rigby, raising cattle and harvesting spuds. He met the love of his life while in high school and married Connie Wheeler shortly after graduation. Together they enjoyed 63 years of glorious marriage, which produced 3 daughters, 3 sons and 25 grandchildren. Their posterity, which at the time of this writing includes 35 great grandchildren, have brought great joy to Dennis and Connie. Connie has been greatly missed since her passing in 2016.

Professionally, Dennis spent twenty-three years in swimming pool construction, eleven years in sales and sales management, and more than twenty years in the financial services business.

In addition to this book, Dennis Boyd Call has written many other "Quick-Read" books that can all be viewed on his website.

<u>www.dennisbcall.com</u>

Dennis authored the exciting novel, "Skullduggery at Quanah" and is also co-author with Denalee Call Chapman of the illustrated children's book, "The Three-Cornered Blanket."

52